THE BASIC SURVIVAL GUIDE TO BEGINNER ICE SKATING

Written By:

Coach Juliana Love

Unless otherwise noted: Scripture taken from the New King James Version. Copyright © 1979, 1980, 1982 by Thomas Nelson, Inc. Used by permission. All rights reserved.

Unless otherwise noted, all quotations and speeches are used by Fair Use or Public Domain

Unless otherwise noted, all poems are written by the author and are copyrighted under Round Top Publishers

Copyright © 2011, 2015 Juliana Love

All rights reserved. No part of this publication may be reproduced, stored in a retrieval system, or transmitted in any form or by any means, electronic, mechanical, photocopying, recording, or otherwise, without the prior written permission of the publisher.

All quotes are in public domain, Brainy quotes, Wikipedia.com

Printed in the United States of America
Website: authorjulianalove.com
Facebook: Author Juliana Love

Round Top Publishers

Juliana Love
P.O. Box 4166
Gettysburg, PA 17325

This book is dedicated to every child, parent of the child, and adult who wants to start out in this amazing world of ice skating; be it for recreation, figure or hockey!

I want to see you succeed, have fun, grow stronger and healthier; to earn the accomplishment and soar with enthusiasm due to each little step of progress you make!

But it starts with a sure and solid foundation!!!

ABOUT THE AUTHOR

I first wrote this book in 2011 when in fact, I was a Figure Skating Coach. It is now October of 2015 and I am no longer coaching. I am working on my own skating instead. I have passed Adult Pre-Bronze and Bronze tests. I am working on passing Silver moves now. I plan to compete in the near future and go as far as I can with my skating. Thank you for taking the time to read this book. I sincerely hope it will help steer you in the right direction. The basics are needed in everything we do!

Happy Skating and please do not give up too soon!

Juliana Love

My family, of course, is dedicated in every book I write.

They are my inspiration.

We have grown as a family due to ice skating and I am forever thankful God sent us to it!

A special thanks to:

Jessica and Nicholas DeTello

Thank you for your help with the pictures!

To my A.C (awesome coach) Justin

Thank you for picking up, where another profoundly great and wonderful coach (Elsabeth) left off!

TABLE OF CONTENTS

PREFACE...................................09

CHAPTER 1

The Rink..................................13

Get Acclimated..............................14

The Scary Zamboni..........................15

The Figure Skate............................16

CHAPTER 2

In the Beginning............................21

The Other Set of Facts.......................24

ABC's or 123's of Ice Skates................26

CHAPTER 3

Group Lessons.................................. 37

CHAPTER 4

Parents.. 47

CHAPTER 5

Hockey.. 55

CHAPTER 6

Special Olympics 61

CHAPTER 7

The Wonderful World of Ice Skating …………..65

AUTHOR BOOKS BY AUTHOR………67

PREFACE

This is the place where I tell you, "This is NOT a "Learn How to Ice Skate Book." I would recommend *"Ice Skating for Dummies."* I read it, studied it and applied it. It is actually a very good book. This book however, is more of a reference guide on the basics of getting to that point. It also contains a great deal of information, where you, the uneducated parent, guardian or birthday party friend, who wants their child or child's friend to ice skate, can reference.

> **Over the years, I have seen parents become increasingly frustrated with the lack of knowledge on how to prepare their child to learn how to ice skate. Some have had to throw them into the pond and watch them either sink or swim. At best, they doggie paddled and at worst, they drowned.**

With the help of this guide I sincerely believe you, the parent, will find some relief. If you will just take the time to read it and actually look through the references, you and your child's skating experience will most definitely be rewarding. With all my heart, the last thing I want is for you to give up prematurely. The world of skating; be it recreation, figure or hockey, is an amazing place to be. This is one of the greatest places to spend quality time with family and friends. It will build sportsmanship and character. It will enhance self-esteem and help secure a positive self-worth. If you have run into the pitfalls of trying to work your way through the maze of ice skating, please read on! This book is designed especially for you.

"I was passionate. I found something that I loved. I could be all alone in a big old skating rink and nobody could get near me and I didn't have to talk to anybody because of my shyness.

It was great. I was in my own fantasy world."

Dorothy Hamill

CHAPTER 1

THE RINK!

The rink can be a maze in itself. Yes! It is cold inside. So please dress accordingly. You would be surprised at how many people ask to turn to the heat on. However, inside where the sheets of ice are, over the bleachers, there should be one or two small heaters that can be turned on by rink staff. Some rinks have two or three sheets of ice. These are usually NHL (National Hockey League) size rinks. Some rink's also have round practice sheets of ice. Inside an ice rink you will or should find the following:

1). Pro Shop where they sell skates and other accessories. It is also where you will pay to skate, unless there is a separate Reception area.

2). Snack Bars or a diner.

3). Locker Rooms

4). Party Rooms

5). Sitting rooms where you can watch your child skate.

6). Offices

7). Small lockers you can pay for while you skate.

8). Skate Rental

9). Some rinks sharpen their own skates and perform maintenance.

10). A Zamboni room! (What's a Zamboni?) A Zamboni is simply an ice machine that re-surfaces the ice. It takes out all the ridges and bumps from

GET ACCLIMATED

It will be of great assistance, if you and your child have never been inside an ice rink that you visit your local rink, BEFORE you sign them up for skating lessons. It is always best to familiarize yourself and your child to the surroundings you will be spending a lot of time at. I know that sounds elementary. Hence the reason this is a "Basic Book." But believe me, it will help. This way, on the first day of lessons, you will know where to go and what to do! I have seen parents bring their child late to class because they had no idea what to do. Then they got mad at the coach because the coach had to start class without them. It wasn't the coach's fault. It was the parents fault. They needed to do what I am telling you now. So please heed the advice, as silly and as small as it is. It will go a long way!

THE SCARY ZAMBONI

Also, to a small child the Zamboni #10 can be pretty intimidating. Don't worry there are no children or adults allowed on the ice while the Zam is in use. However, if time permits, you might want to let your child watch it cut the ice. This will help get the child used to the size, the sound, and the purpose of the machine. It will help them to understand the different textures of the ice as well. Bumpy ice is dangerous to skate on, and precisely why it is why it is necessary to resurface it, or clean it. This allows the ice to become smooth again.

While skating on ice that had several large holes and ruts, due to the size of my toe picks, once my skate crossed over a rut, it dug into the ice and down I went. Three years later, I finally recovered from one of the worst injuries I have ever had – a shoulder injury. Yet, at no time was I ever upset with the rink. We, the skaters, skate at our own risk.

THE FIGURE SKATE

This is where I would briefly like to talk about the figure skate. Most rinks use these for Group Lessons. The reason being, it helps to work on edges. Toe picks are for the purpose of jumping, some spinning such as pivots, as well as other things. If you don't know how to use a toe pick and lean forward on your toes, you probably will stop short and fall. This is common and eventually stops once you get used to proper balance on your blades. But, even an experienced skater like myself, once my toe pick dug into a rut that was approximately half an inch deep, I could not stop myself from going down. This is not to deter you from wanting to ice skate or to learn the sports of figure skating and ice hockey. It is just to let you know, like any other sport, the chance for injury is possible. But with the basic steps, injuries in most cases are preventable.

"When I'm on the ice, it's my domain. It's what I love doing. It's where I love to be"

Elizabeth Manley

CHAPTER 2

IN THE BEGINNING!

As a figure skater myself, it ALWAYS amazes me when I see children and adults on the ice with the wrong size skates, or skates that are not laced right.

> **Seriously folks, that is like trying to row a boat with a Popsicle stick.**

You won't get very far, and you will either get hurt, or tire yourself out to the point you won't want to ever get in that boat again, all with good reason. Ice skating is not supposed to be a chore. Let me repeat that.

ICE SKATING
IS NOT SUPPOSED TO BE A CHORE!!!

It isn't like washing dishes or taking out the trash. Ice skating is a fascinating sport, full of beauty, grace and free flowing stress relief. Now for those of you who are leaning towards hockey, I will get to that. If there is beauty and grace on the hockey side of ice skating, we have a problem! However, whether you are skating for recreation, figure or hockey, everyone needs to start at the basics. The most basic of all, are your ice skates.

Parents, this survival guide is especially designed for you, who have no idea about the fundamentals of ice skating. So, let's define the word "fundamental." The word is defined as, "basic, primary and elementary." Our children cannot graduate to middle school if they have failed elementary school, right? The basics are essential to building a solid foundation. The last thing we want is for your child to fall through thin ice, symbolically speaking. We want their foundation on the ice to be solid, strong and without cracks. If they have on the wrong size skates, they are doomed to fall and/or fail, it's guaranteed. Planned failure is the worst kind of failure!

I have seen over and over again parents who have no knowledge about this sport and turn their kids loose out on the ice. Let's talk about this from a child's point of view shall we? Here is the scenario. Group Lessons…It is like their worst nightmare coming true. They have on the wrong size skates and they are stuck in a group without mommy and daddy, and they can barely stand up. They are scared. They are in pain. They are thrown into a cave full of scary monsters and all they want to do is run away. But they can't. Why? Because they can't even walk right. You spent around 100$ for these lessons and you are upset because your child isn't having fun and isn't making any progress. Well no wonder…! They have on poor fitting skates and they cannot keep up with their class.

THE OTHER SET OF FACTS

NOW...a good coach will recognize the problem and immediately inform you, the parent to change their skates. But this is where I also must in all honesty state the other set of facts. Not all coaches will check to see if your child has on the right skates and that folks is my biggest pet peeve in ice skating. For instance, I saw a coach trying to coerce a student (now bear in mind, someone had to pay the coach for this lesson), but the coach kept trying to leer the child away from the wall, which at some point needs to happen, because truthfully, "The wall is not your friend." It is in fact, more of a deterrent.

But before we can get the kids or adults away from the wall, we must first make sure they can at the very least stand upright. Anyway, back to this poor kid grabbing onto the wall for dear life. Well, it took me a second as I skated by her on my merry way to look down and see the problem. Her skates were too big, not only that they were not even tied right. It is a difficult position to be put in. There are all kinds of rules a coach must follow as to not step over the boundaries or on the toes of the other coach. It is for the sake of the skater that I decided to write this book. After all, without the skater, there is no one to coach!

So, as much as I would like to commend every ice skating coach, I simply cannot. Parents please do not leave the fate of your child solely up to the coaches. It is your responsibility to see to it that your child is properly fitted. After all, someone had to pay for the ice time as well as the coach giving the lesson. Why do you want to waste your money and not see your child have a good time?

Proper fitting skates are the first essential in ice skating. Even if you cannot afford right away to buy your child their own skates, proper fitting rental skates are just as important, if not more important because every week they will end up with a different pair of skates. At least getting them fitted by a trained professional, you will know what size skate to rent. So, after having said all of that, here are the ABC'S or rather the

123's of ice skates and what you need to do to make sure your child is properly fitted.

ABC'S OR 123'S OF ICE SKATES

1). I suggest first and foremost you have your child fitted for skates, by a professional. Let me point out, AGAIN, most coaches are not trained to fit ice skates. If there is a Pro Shop in your rink, you should have trained and experienced staff to assist you. This needs to happen BEFORE your child takes his or her first step on ice.

It is dangerous to put your child out on ice with the wrong size skates.

See if you can make an appointment with someone, as it takes about 30 minutes to properly fit someone for skates. This doesn't mean you have to buy them right away.

However, it will help you know the correct size to get at Skate Rental. However, please make sure you are making the staff aware you or your child needs to be fitted for rented skates, if you are not buying new skates right away. The sizes could vary. So please make sure you specify.

I have seen parents get different sizes every week. That is very detrimental because it changes balance and posture at every lesson. So, the child has to adjust and then re-adjust. If new skates cannot be afforded at the time, once your child is properly fitted for rentals, try to make sure they have the same size skate from Skate Rental.

2). If there is not a Pro Shop at your rink, perhaps you can find one in your area that does. If there isn't one close by, perhaps your rink has a mat that your child can stand on, so that you know what size skate to use at Skate Rental. Typically, skates are a size smaller then our shoe size. I wear a size 8 shoe and my skates are size 7. If a Pro Shop is not available and a mat isn't either, then start screaming.

Someone will surely come running to help you! Haha..just kidding.

But seriously! The staff at the Skate Rental do not usually inform you, the uninformed parent of the child, or the adult skating, the in's and out's of ice skates. They just ask your size and give you whatever you tell them. When you cannot walk a straight line and wobble like you are drunk, then something is seriously wrong. If you are wobbling like that on a dry ground, think of what an ice cold, slippery surface is going to do. Sorry! But this is really what happens day after day. I do not understand it and I NEVER will.

> **Please for the safety of your child and/or for yourself, it is imperative that the right size skates are worn.**

3).We need to talk about lacing the skates. Now that you have the right size, if you don't lace them right, you are still paddling that boat with a Popsicle Stick. See picture **#1** on the following page.

Do you see how aligned the laces are where they cross over in the center? That is how a laced up skate should look up to that point. Once you lace them and just before the eyelets, you want to now tie it like a regular shoe lace, crossing over and under and pulling the two strings tight. See picture **#1** on the following page.

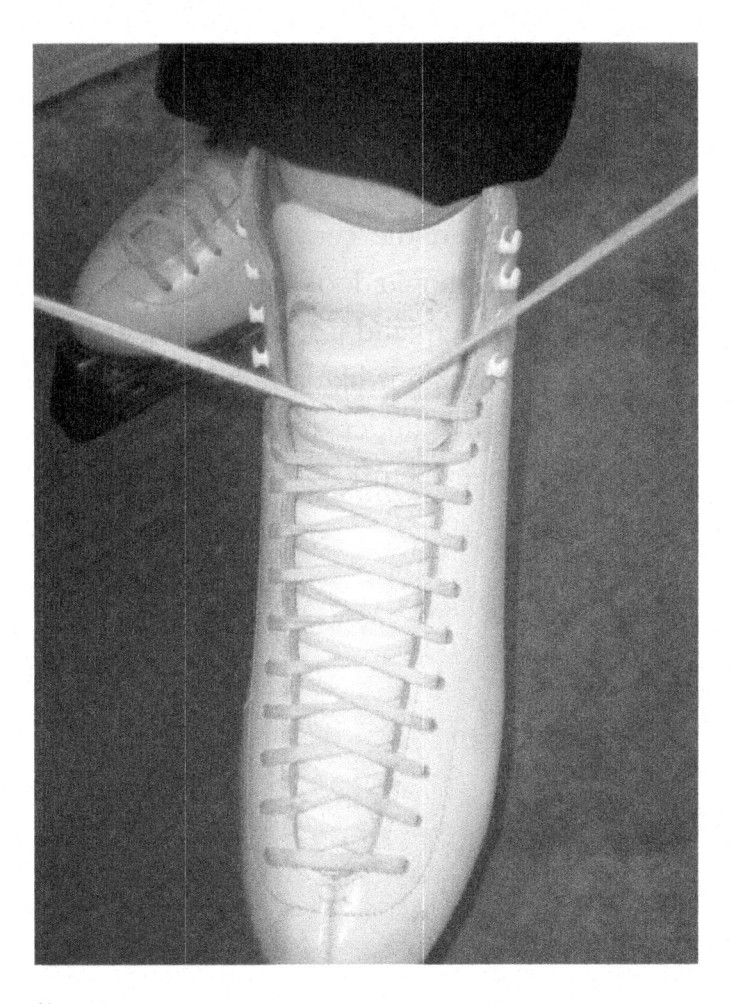

#1

Now, after you have crossed over the laces, you are now ready to tie up the rest of the skate. Most people think to tie the eyelets in an upward motion. You actually want to tie them in a downward motion. This helps to keep the laces in place. See picture **#2** below.

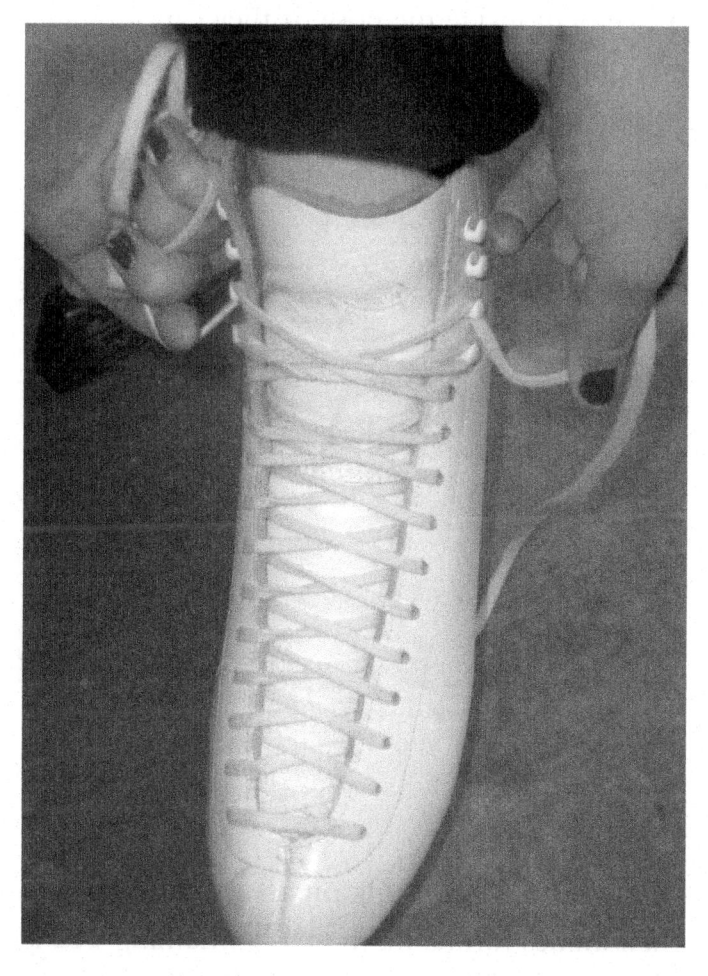

#2

If your child is walking on top of the blade, like they are walking normal, with minimal movement inside the boot, if they can walk in a straight line without wobbling, your child should be good to go. See picture **#3**

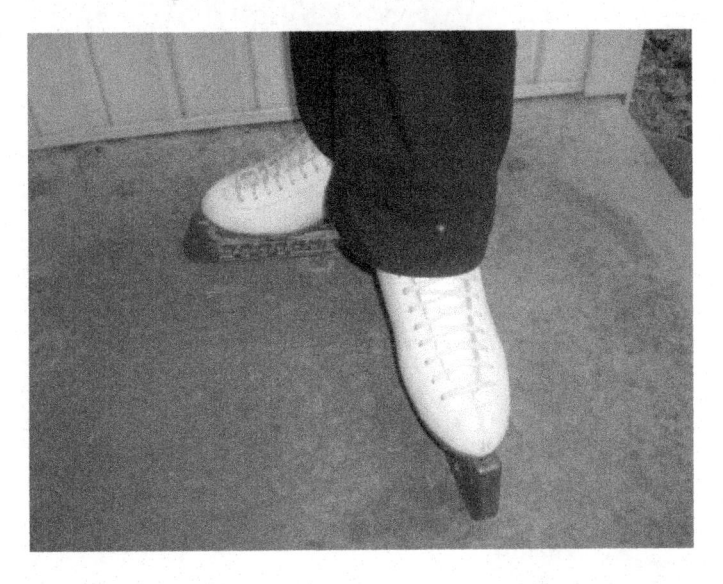

 # 3

If your child is walking on an inside edge, with their ankles turned in, there is something wrong and your child's skates need to be looked at. Please see picture **#4** on the following page.

#4

Sometimes it is necessary to add additional soles and support for your skates. If you are using rented skates, it is usually not possible to add these. If you are serious about skating, whether for your child or if you're an adult, it is always best to buy your own skates. This allows your feet to mold itself into the skate. It should feel as if you aren't wearing any skates. They should be that comfortable. It should feel as if you are wearing gloves on your feet. Skates that are too tight, try to re-lace the skates. There should be no movement inside the skate, other than the ability to wiggle toes. We don't want to cut off the circulation, I mean what would be the point in that? That would totally defeat the purpose as with no circulation, our feet would fall off!

In terms of socks, I skate barefoot. So, I cannot advise you on that. It is just whatever works best for your child, or for any adult reading this who wants to skate. But there again, try to stay consistent with the socks. In other words, if you start with thin socks and this is working, don't use thicker socks the following week. You will find your feet hurting pretty badly!

"Figure skating is theatrical. It's artistic. It's elegant. It's extremely athletic. And there's a very specific audience for that."

Johnny Weir

CHAPTER 3

GROUP LESSONS!

> **Parents, as a coach, please understand my heart in this. Unless you have had to teach twelve students at one time, you have no idea how difficult it can be.**
>
> **Please be patient with us!**

PSA stands for "Professional Skaters Association." Their website is www.skatepsa.com. They are responsible for training "quality" coaches. Those of us who are hired at a PSA rated rink, must adhere to certain guidelines and continuing education credits. Most coaches also have training in Sports Safety as well, that does include First Aid and CPR for Coaches. If after the first class your child hasn't moved across the ice yet, please do not be discouraged.

I had a student who graduated from another class. The first time I saw him, I noticed his skates were too big. This is why I suggest you:

PLEASE take the time to get your child properly fitted before any lessons.

Hopefully you will read it enough so it gets down in your subconscious and even hear it in your sleep!

But just know I would NOT be this adamant if I did not care!

Unfortunately, there are some coaches, even PSA rated, who will miss the fact that their student isn't wearing the right skates. But, this child the following week had on new hockey skates. Wow, he skated worse than he did with the wrong rental skates. The parents were somewhat distraught. I knew it would work out for the best, as the following week, he skated like a pro! Well, at least a new beginner hockey pro! Let me interject something here.

> **NORMALLY hockey skates are not permitted in the Learn to Skate Classes until a child has reached a Basic Level 3.**

This is to ensure that proper edges are taught using figure skates. Hockey skates do not have toe-picks and the edges are sharpened differently than figure skates. It takes time to break in new skates, whether hockey or figure.

> **But, parents, if you see your little Joe or your little Sally crying, please understand something, we are aware of it.**
>
> **It isn't that we are ignoring your child.**

There are times when we have to turn our attention to the other students. We cannot give all our attention to your crying child. I understand that sounds harsh. It isn't meant to be. It just means, we don't want you going off the deep end, banging on the boards trying to get us to react to your child. I promise you, your child will be tended to. We don't want you feeling as if you are not getting your money's worth. We have to handle each child differently. Some children just need a hug. Some just need a wave to mom or dad. But there are some kids who do throw temper tantrums on the ice and at times it is best to skate away until they are finished, or to remove them from the ice.

But please give us the benefit of the doubt. We are there to assist and train your children. I had a child crying that at other lessons was my best student. When I skated over to him, he started crying hysterically. I asked him what was wrong and he couldn't tell me. I asked him if he could skate for a minute, and as he began to, the tears kept coming. I asked him then to wave to his mom. It was at that point, she waved me to bring him. It was necessary for me to escort her son off the ice. I simply had the class skate another lap of, "March, march, glide." Apparently, this little boy wasn't feeling well. We are not babysitters. But we do care about our students. The last thing we want is for your child to be unhappy, in pain and not feeling well.

I know as loving parents that it is hard to restrain yourself if you feel your child is being left out. But, please just give it some time. If you feel **after** the second or third class that your child is not being treated right, then by all means talk to the Skating Director. But with only one or two classes, it isn't realistic to complain. It takes at least those two classes for the coach to understand your child's skating level. The students are also learning about the coach. Just don't freak out on us and tell us goodbye! That is doing your child a great injustice. Also, it is your responsibility to get your child to practice sessions. Some rinks offer free Public Session passes for every Group Session. This will help your child get used to the ice. You are spending money on their lessons. Take advantage of anything offered for free (except anything illegal of course)!

You can look up information for the Learn to Skate Lessons on the United States Figure Skating website. Their website is www.usfsa.org. There is a whole lot of necessary information you can find, and you can also become a member of both PSA and USFS. If you are serious about figure skating whether for yourself, or for your child, than you should become a member of at least United States Figure Skating Association or your local Figure Skating Club. The clubs typically give you a membership to USFS and they have so much to offer. Check out your local club for more information. I used to think there was a great deal of information at the book stores about figure skating. But there are very few beginner survival guides like this one. There are however, parent guides, coaches guides on the PSA website and on the USFS

> **Just take some time to get educated. The worst thing you can do is not know what is going on inside the rink or on the ice.**

You need to know what your child is getting involved in. You need to know what you are getting yourself involved in as well. Group Lessons could take your child to the Olympics. It is possible. However, the amount of commitment involved is overwhelming. Yet, to see your child smile after his or first competition, is a glorious thing. To see them in their costumes accomplishing a jump or spin, and wooing the judges and audience, is well worth it. Mind you, this is a competitive sport. Not every child with Olympic potential will make it. There will be ups and down, bumps and bruises for sure. Yet, each accomplishment builds for the next one.

"Before I go onto the ice, my coach helps me get focused.

He takes me through the routine until I'm ready to go out."

Sarah Schmidek

CHAPTER 4

PARENTS!

Okay! Let's get real shall we? Since I have lured you in with all of this ice skating information, it is at this point, I MUST ask the question.

> **Are you trying to live your figure skating or hockey dream through your child? If so, you are making everybody miserable.**

I have seen some parents act worse than a gang of monkeys fighting over bunch of bananas. It truly is a sad thing to behold. I have seen fathers scream at their sons for not playing well at a hockey game. I have seen these same kids reduced to tears because of the embarrassment they feel. Fathers and mothers, if you cannot handle the slightest failure on your child's part, stay out of the rink! Our kids are just that, our kids. They are not our trophies. They are not on display. Let me at this time kindly direct you to the **Character Counts** website….www.charactercounts.org! It might help you learn some manners! I know the truth hurts. But deal with it! I hate to see these kids get degraded in front of other team mates and other people. Give your child some dignity and respect. They have coaches who are there to coach them. If they have a problem with their performance, it is their job to "coach" them. I have seen parents from the bleachers cussing out refs as well. SAY WHAT? We don't need to cuss at anybody. FOR REAL! We need to be like…role models!

Okay true confessions. Have I ever cussed out one of those refs while watching one of my sons' hockey games? Well, I cannot say I have ever actually cussed. Have I yelled at the ref's, without cussing, "Yes." So just for the record, I have never been thrown out of a game for cussing out a ref. Have I ever come close to it? I won't go there. This is supposed to be me talking about being a role model!

> However, I have **NEVER** not even once, yelled at my sons' for not playing good enough. They have coaches as I have already stated that do enough hooting and hollering. They don't need me adding to it. To be perfectly honest, your child doesn't need you yelling at him or her either, especially **IN FRONT OF OTHER KIDS!** How totally degrading to your child and how totally embarrassing for him or her. Please refrain yourself from any such behavior.

It is here I must confess again. I am a truthful kind of a woman who hides nothing. While watching my son's hockey team play, a coach on an opposing team yelled out, "You suck! Get that piece of trash off the ice." This coach was referring to a high school student who just checked one of his players. Okay! So for those of you with inquiring minds, I simply lost it. I didn't cuss. But I made my presence known as (an off ice mom). The entire game, I yelled out to the coach, banged on the boards, went crazy every time our team scored a goal and after the game, confronted the coach. Regardless if it was an isolated incident or not, coaches are supposed to be role models, have self-control, and remember the codes and ethics they are certified under. I have been around the ice a very long time, and still am dumbfounded at such a despicable display of un-sportsman like conduct coming from a coach and it wasn't even my kid he said those things to. But that was not the point. It was minor child being verbally assaulted by someone who was certified by USA Hockey.

> **Coaches need to make sure they remember if a child cannot trust even them to act accordingly, then why should they?**
>
> **Just saying!**

It is called Responsible Coaching, and you will find the information in regard to that on the USA Hockey website… www.usahockey.com!

"You miss 100% of the shots you never take."

Wayne Gretzky

CHAPTER 5

HOCKEY!

> **Well, if you are seriously interested in having your child skate on an ice hockey team, the first thing I would suggest is that you make sure your child can skate.**

OUCH! I know...this doesn't get any easier for me either!!! Parents, I greatly advise your child reach a Basic Level 3 before you try to enroll them in a hockey program. Most rinks with hockey programs do not allow children to be enrolled unless they are at least a Basic Level 3. They have enough to deal with. With all that gear, the last thing they need is to skate bad. What a mess! It is bad enough dealing with the pressure of learning how to play the game, but, dear God if they can't even skate. You have not only taken away the popsicle stick, you have proceeded to remove the boat as well! Give your child some slack will you. I know this sounds crazy. But, this actually happens. There are kids on teams who cannot skate! Let's stop putting the cart before the horse, shall we. Give the horse the chance to succeed, instead of causing him to fail right from the gate. Your child doesn't need to hear the words, "you suck." Sorry! But this is the real world. Give your child a chance to succeed at one of the greatest sports in the world. Let them skate for themselves, and not for your own ego. You are not the one out there on that ice. Yet, you should be their greatest sense of support and comfort.

So, let's talk about hockey for a moment. I can't. I have no idea! I am not a hockey coach. I am, however, a Hockey Development Ice Skating Coach. In other words, I generally coach kids that already are on hockey teams who just need some extra help with skating. It is a whole different ball game when you add all that hockey equipment. Hockey Development skating classes, help add the gear to the skates and the kids I have taught in this class, have all shown great improvement on their teams.

I do, however, also suggest you go to the ww.usahockey.com website. There you will find an enormous about of much needed information on the ins and outs of hockey! Also, chances are you have a Hockey Director at your rink. Talk to him. Talk to other parents and coaches. See what you can do get involved and to volunteer your time. It keeps you in the loop instead of outside it getting dizzy wondering what the heck is going on!!!

Parents, can I also just say this…! I know you have to work. I know you might not be at every game. Just try to be at most of the games. I heard one player tell me,

> *"I wish my dad was here. He is never here. He has to work all the time."*

I started to cry for him right in the Penalty Box. My heart broke for him. My older son didn't have a dad. In order for me to afford the Hockey fees, I had to work extra at the ice rink. I didn't mind doing odd jobs, like the snack bar and skate rental, (this was besides all of my coaching). But, at least I went the extra mile so that my boys could play. I was at every game and this at times was with chronic pain! My boys have my total support. I washed jerseys, worked the Penalty Box, sewed letters and worked the bake table. I have most definitely worn myself out. I had taken on at times more then what I could chew and almost choked.

However, my boys can look back and know that I was there for them. They know I love them. They know how important they are to me and it is my pleasure to see them succeed. Please understand I am not patting myself on the back. I am simply stating facts. If you can, support your child at every cost. I realize (again) you have to work. But if at all possible, try to make it a game or two. Our kids play better when they have our support. Even big tough seniors, need support. So, don't let their age fool you. Just know they need you!

I would like to bring something to the sport, to somehow change it for the better and make a difference, not just bring home medals."

Jayson Dénommée

CHAPTER 6

SPECIAL OLYMPICS!

This is a subject near and dear to my heart, as I teach ice skating for Special Olympics. I cannot tell you how blessed I am to be allowed to do this. I teach Special Olympics for free and the ice time is also free, due to the generosity of the General Manager. As a woman with disabilities myself, I know firsthand how incredibly therapeutic ice skating can be. When I am ice skating for myself, or coaching, it is rare that I feel pain. I live in chronic pain otherwise. I didn't start ice skating again until well after my accident and it has given me a way to keep myself fit.

If you have a son or daughter with disabilities, please don't count out ice skating.

It is very possible this sport will work for your child. Check out your local rink to see if they offer Special Olympics and if they don't, perhaps you can start the program with an interested coach! The reason a lot of parents don't try ice skating for their child with disabilities, more often than not, is because the program isn't offered! So, please check to see if you can get a program going, if one isn't started already. Also, there are "Special Hockey Teams." You can check out the website at specialusahockey.com!

"Continuous effort – not strength or intelligence is the key to unlocking your potential."

Liane Carlos

CHAPTER SEVEN

WONDERFUL WORLD of ICE SKATING

Though this has been a very brief journey, I hope it has helped even in the smallest of measures. After seeing firsthand the realities of the lack of basic preparation for ice skating, as an author, I just couldn't help myself. I had to write this guide. If it has helped you or your child in anyway, and you would like to contact me, feel free to email me at:

juliana.everwood@gmail.com

Take care and I sincerely hope you come to love the wonderful world of ice skating as much as I do.

Coach Juliana Love

AUTHOR'S OTHER BOOKS

SUMMER RAY SERIES

Volume 1 – This Fair and Blighted Land

Volume 2 – Savannah's Calling

Volume 3 – Her Yankee Heart

Volume 4 – The Journey Home

Volume 5 – Time...Begins Again

Volume 6 – The Other Side of Time

Summer Ray No Matter What!

The Power of Purpose

I Defied...Suicide

The Process of Empowerment

They Laughed At Noah...Till It Rained

The Blessings of Liberty

Detox…The Deceit, Damage, Devil and Doom

150th Battle of Gettysburg; Special Photography Edition

ALL BOOKS CAN BE BOUGHT VIA

AMAZON.COM

Lightning Source UK Ltd.
Milton Keynes UK
UKOW01f1956301017
311910UK00009B/574/P